StoryTime & Mor

Treasures

PRIMARY READER STUDY GUIDE FOR A COLLECTION OF STORIES

TEACHER KEY

Little Bear
Little Bear's Visit
Caps for Sale
Blueberries for Sal
Make Way for Ducklings
Billy and Blaze
Blaze and the Forest Fire
The Story About Ping
Keep the Lights Burning, Abbie
Stone Soup
The Little House
Miss Rumphius

STORYTIME TREASURES
AND
MORE STORYTIME TREASURES

Primary Reader Study Guide
Teacher Key

Published by:
Memoria Press
www.memoriapress.com

ISBN #978-1-61538-030-5

Cover Illustration by Starr L. Steinbach
Cover Design & Interior Illustration by Karah J. Force

StoryTime Treasures

TABLE OF CONTENTS

Study Guide pp. 6-9

Lesson 1: What Will Little Bear Wear?
(reading pages 11-21)

Say each word. Write it. Use it in a sentence.

Answers will vary.

Read each sentence. What does the bold word mean?

1. shout of joy
2. animal hair

Fill in the blanks or answer in complete sentences.

1. Little Bear was cold.
2. Hat, coat, snow pants
3. His own fur made him the warmest.
4. I, cold

Let's Learn.

1. The snow is cold and white.
2. A bear has a fur coat.

Just for Fun

Study Guide pp. 10-13

Lesson 2: Birthday Soup
(reading pages 22-35)

Say each word. Write it. Use it in a sentence.

Answers will vary.

Read each sentence. What does the bold word mean?

1. vegetables
2. close

Answer in complete sentences.

1. Little Bear made Birthday Soup.
2. He put them in the big black pot.
3. She was making his birthday cake.

Let's Learn.

1. Period
2. Question mark
3. Question mark
4. Period

Just for Fun

3 1 2

Study Guide pp. 14-16

Lesson 3: Little Bear Goes to the Moon
(reading pages 36-48)

Say each word. Write it. Use it in a sentence.

Answers will vary.

Read each sentence. What does the bold word mean?

1. do not
2. hard hat worn for protection

Fill in the blanks or answer in complete sentences.

1. He told her he was going to the moon.
2. a little tree on a little hill
3. He meant, "Stop being silly."
4. nap

Just for Fun

Answers will vary.

Study Guide pp. 17-21

Lesson 4: Little Bear's Wish
(reading pages 50-63)

Say each word. Write it. Use it in a sentence.

Answers will vary.

Read each sentence. What does the bold word mean?

1. passageway
2. cannot

Answer in complete sentences.

1. Little Bear was wishing.
2. He would go all the way to China.
3. He would drive a big red car.
4. He wished he could hear stories of what he once did.

Something to Do

Answers will vary.

Let's Learn.

1. My sister has a new doll.
2. She named the doll Emma.
3. The doll is from China.

Just for Fun

Answers will vary.

Study Guide pp. 24-27

Lesson 1: Grandmother and Grandfather Bear
(reading pages 9-23)

Say each word. Write it. Use it in a sentence.

Answers will vary.

Read each sentence. What does the bold word mean?

1. naughty elf
2. dance

Fill in the blanks or answer in complete sentences.

1. They lived in a little house in the woods.
2. look at all the nice things.
3. Liked, big, hat, Look, at, me
4. He told Little Bear not to make Grandfather tired.

Let's Learn.

jumped looked laughed cooked

Just for Fun

Answers will vary.

Study Guide pp. 28-30

Lesson 2: Mother Bear's Robin
(reading pages 24-41)

Say each word. Write it. Use it in a sentence.

Answers will vary.

Read each sentence. What does the bold word mean?

1. around
2. grandchildren

Answer in complete sentences.

1. She found a baby robin.
2. Mother Bear put it by the window.
3. The robin was sad because it could not sing or fly inside the house.
4. She set him free.

Just for Fun

Study Guide pp. 31-35

Lesson 3: Goblin Story
(reading pages 42-54)

Say each word. Write it. Use it in a sentence.

Answers will vary.

Read each sentence. What does the bold word mean?

1. laughed softly
2. that is

Answer in complete sentences.

1. The goblin heard something go bump.
2. His shoes went "pit-pat-pit-pat."
3. He hid in a hole in a tree.
4. His shoes did not want to stay behind.

Something to Do

Answers will vary.

Let's Learn.

1. old, cold, dark
2. brown, furry, curious
3. crisp, sweet, red

Just for Fun

Answers will vary.

Study Guide pp. 36-39

Lesson 4: Not Tired
(reading pages 56-64)

Say each word. Write it. Use it in a sentence.

Answers will vary.

Read each sentence. What does the bold word mean?

1. couch
2. young bear

Fill in the blanks or answer in complete sentences.

1. He was waiting for Mother Bear and Father Bear to come home.
2. He said he would take Little Bear fishing.
3. good, clever
4. He fell fast asleep.

Just for Fun

Answers will vary.

Study Guide pp. 42-45

Lesson 1
Read through "And what do you think he saw?"

Say each word. Write it. Use it in a sentence.

Answers will vary.

Read each sentence. What does the bold word mean?

1. turn over or spill
2. area away from the city
3. full of energy again

Fill in the blanks or answer in complete sentences.

1. The peddler sold caps.
2. He carried them on top of his head.
3. along, Caps, sale, cents
4. He couldn't sell any caps.
5. He rested under a great big tree.

Just for Fun

Answers will vary.

Cap Math

Use the number words to fill in the answers below.

1. four	4. four
2. four	5. four
3. zero	6. one

Use numerals to fill in the answers below.

1. $4 + 4 = 8$
2. $0 + 4 = 4$
3. $4 + 1 = 5$
4. 17

Study Guide pp. 46-49

Lesson 2
Read from "On every branch ..." to the end.

Say each word. Write it. Use it in a sentence.

Answers will vary.

Read each sentence. What does the bold word mean?

1. at last
2. did not
3. "No, no, no."

Answer in complete sentences.

1. The peddler saw monkeys.
2. Every monkey was wearing a cap.
3. He spoke to the monkeys.
4. The peddler felt angry.
5. They were copying the peddler.

Past Tense

called told

Write the present tense of the verb.

shake	sit	shout
make	see	look
speak	throw	stamp

Just for Fun

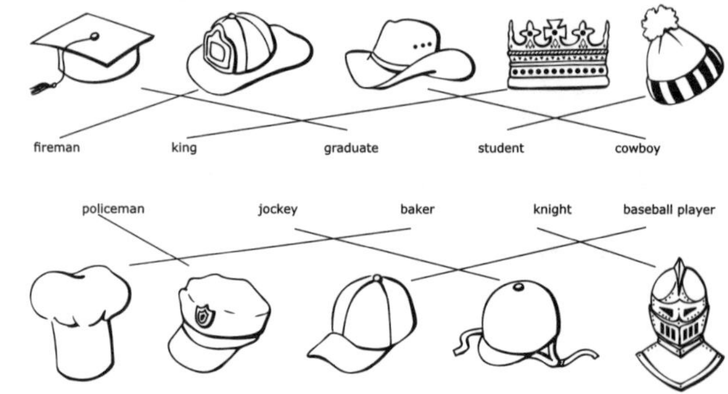

Study Guide pp. 52-55

Lesson 1

Read through "... sat down right in the middle and ate blueberries."

Say each word. Write it. Use it in a sentence.

Answers will vary.

Read each sentence. What does the bold word mean?

1. seal in a jar for later
2. the sound of berries hitting the bottom of the pail
3. bunch, group

Answer in complete sentences.

1. They wanted to can the berries to have food for the winter.
2. Little Sal kept eating the berries she picked.
3. It made no sound because the bottom of the pail was already covered with berries.
4. They wanted to grow big and fat to store up food for the long, cold winter.
5. Little Bear kept stopping to eat the berries.

Language Lesson

1. **"**We will take our berries home and can them,**"** said her mother. **"**Then we will have food for the winter.**"**
2. Her mother stopped picking and said, **"**Now, Sal, you run along and pick your own berries.**"**
3. **"**Little Bear,**"** she said, **"**eat lots of berries and grow big and fat.**"**
4. She heard a noise from around a rock and thought, **"**That is my mother walking along!**"**
5. They stopped eating berries and flew away, saying, **"**Caw, Caw, Caw.**"**

Study Guide pp. 56-59

Lesson 2

Read through "... all mixed up with each other among the blueberries on Blueberry Hill."

Say each word. Write it. Use it in a sentence.

Answers will vary.

Read each sentence. What does the bold word mean?

1. began walking
2. walking with heavy steps
3. type of bird

Fill in the blanks or answer in complete sentences.

1. She had eaten all of the berries she could reach from where she was sitting.
2. She heard a noise coming from the other side of the rock, so she thought it was her mother.
3. The crows said, "Caw, Caw, Caw" as they flew away.
4. Little Sal tramped right along beside Little Bear's mother.
5. Bear, Sal, mixed

Just for Fun

Study Guide pp. 60-63

Lesson 3

Read to the end of the book.

Say each word. Write it. Use it in a sentence.

Answers will vary.

Read each sentence. What does the bold word mean?

1. nonsense word imitating the sound of choking
2. walked quietly up
3. spoken breathlessly in shock

Answer in complete sentences.

1. Little Bear's mother heard Little Sal walking along behind.
2. She turned around to see what on earth could make a noise like *kuplunk!*
3. She heard Little Bear tramping along behind.
4. Little Bear padded up and peeked into her pail.
5. She was afraid of bears.

Language Lesson

1. kuplunk
2. kuplink
3. Caw, Caw, Caw
4. munch, munch; gulp
5. Garumpf

Study Guide pp. 66-69

esson 1
ead through "... called on Michael every day."

Say each word. Write it. Use it in a entence.

nswers will vary.

Read each sentence. What does the bold word mean?

. was good for
. fond of himself
. fearful and trembling
. lose feathers

Answer in complete sentences.

. They were looking for a place to live.
. It was not a real bird.
. It was unsafe because of people riding bicycles.
. They were beginning to molt.
. Michael fed them peanuts.

anguage Lesson

. Dogwood Rd.
. Dr. Brown
. Mrs. Newman
. Mr. Crumb
. Main St.
. Longest Dr.

Study Guide pp. 70-73

Lesson 2
Read through "... blowing his whistle."

Say each word. Write it. Use it in a sentence.

Answers will vary.

Read each sentence. What does the bold word mean?

1. important job
2. happy
3. land on the other side of the pond

Fill in the blanks or answer in complete sentences.

1. She had to sit on her eggs to keep them warm.
2. Jack, Kack, Lack, Mack, Ouack, Pack, and Quack are the names of the ducklings.
3. The ducks quacked at the honking cars.
4. Michael, arms, whistle

Language Lesson*

1. cold, fold, hold, gold, sold, told
2. ball, call, fall, hall, tall, wall
3. beat, heat, meat, neat, seat, wheat

**(Answers will vary)*

Study Guide pp. 74-79

Lesson 3
Read to the end of the book.

Say each word. Write it. Use it in a sentence.

Answers will vary.

Read each sentence. What does the bold word mean?

1. stood firmly
2. work station (small boxlike room with telephone)
3. slang for 'isn't'

Answer in complete sentences.

1. He stopped traffic so that the ducks could safely cross the road.
2. He called to tell them there was a family of ducks walking down the street.
3. She tipped her nose in the air and walked along with an extra swing in her waddle.
4. Mr. Mallard was waiting for them.
5. They follow the swan boats and eat peanuts.

Just for Fun

Answers will vary.

MORE STORYTIME TREASURES

Study Guide pp. 6-9

Lesson 1
(reading pages 1-22)

Say each word. Write it. Use it in a sentence.

Answers will vary.

Read each sentence. What does the bold word mean?

1. grass
2. reddish-brown
3. a stripe on the face of an animal

Fill in the blanks or answer in complete sentences.

1. Billy loves horses.
2. He was a beautiful bay pony with four white feet and a white nose.
3. start, pony, like, each, other
4. He knew there would be a carrot or a piece of sugar, as well as much petting.

Fill in the circle beside the correct answer.

1. prancing pony
2. thinking for a long time
3. a flashlight
4. go for a long ride with Blaze
5. both of these things

Art Activity

1. rabbits
2. a squirrel
3. a bird and its nest
4. a stone wall
5. rocks
6. trees
7. grass
8. a path

Study Guide pp. 10-13

Lesson 2
(reading pages 24-48)

Say each word. Write it. Use it in a sentence.

Answers will vary.

Read each sentence. What does the bold word mean?

1. crying out
2. wrapped (with a strip of material)
3. happily

Answer in complete sentences.

1. The dog was caught in a trap.
2. He usually slept in the stable with Blaze.
3. He felt afraid that he would not win.
4. Rex was jumping beside him.
5. He carried his head very high and pranced

Now You Try It!

a flower	**an** insect	**an** earthworm
an idea	**an** ocean	**a** catfish
a cloud	**a** wagon	**a** hammer
a snowflake	**a** puzzle	**an** alligator

a funny clown	**an** ugly bug	**a** friendly dog
a red cherry	**a** cozy bed	**an** orderly desk

Study Guide pp. 16-19

Lesson 1
(reading pages 1-22)

Say each word. Write it. Use it in a sentence.

Answers will vary.

Read each sentence. What does the bold word mean?

1. force
2. the ground at the edge of the brook crumbled
3. a. moving quickly
   b. very upsetting

Fill in the blanks or answer in complete sentences.

1. Rex, them, rides, sick, mother, home, day, ride, little, winding, woods
2. There was a danger of starting a forest fire.
3. He wanted to save the woods so he went quickly for help.
4. high stone wall, brook, high wall with barbed wire at the top

Sentence Types

1. **E** It is freezing cold out here!
2. **I** Do you need a jacket?
3. **D** My mittens keep my hands warm.
4. **I** Can we build a snowman?
5. **D** The sun is coming out.
6. **E** Our snowman is going to melt!

Study Guide pp. 20-23

Lesson 2
(reading pages 24-48)

Say each word. Write it. Use it in a sentence.

Answers will vary.

Read each sentence. What does the bold word mean?

1. back
2. with much trying
3. knock

Answer in complete sentences.

1. Blaze galloped bravely.
2. The farmhouse was across the field.
3. The farmer's wife called the neighbors.
4. "You're the best pony in the world, Blaze–the very best!"
5. The box that came for Billy had a bridle, a headband, and a pair of boots inside.

Nouns

1. **P** Sleeping Beauty
2. **C** farmer
3. **P** Mount Evergreen
4. **C** boy
5. **C** baker
6. **P** Shoe Mart
7. **P** Uncle Joe
8. **C** bird

1. Emily
2. Willow Road
3. dog
4. ring (leave as is)

Study Guide pp. 26-29

Lesson 1
(reading pages 2-10)

Say each word. Write it. Use it in a sentence.

Answers will vary.

Read each sentence. What does the bold word mean?

1. watching, knowing
2. good
3. running with light steps

Answer in complete sentences.

1. Their home was a boat on the Yangtze River.
2. "La-la-la-la-lei!"
3. The last duck would receive a spank on the back.
4. Ping was fishing with his head underwater.
5. He did not want to be spanked.
6. Ping slept near the grasses on the bank of the river.

Some Things to Talk About

Ping, Mother, Father, 2 sisters, 3 brothers, 11 aunts, 7 uncles, and 42 cousins = ***68*** ducks in Ping's family.

1. Asia
2. Beijing
3. Chinese

Study Guide pp. 30-33

Lesson 2
(reading pages 11-22)

Say each word. Write it. Use it in a sentence.

Answers will vary.

Read each sentence. What does the bold word mean?

1. rushing, moving quickly
2. soft
3. quickly grabbed

Fill in the blanks or answer in complete sentences.

1. 1. fishing
   2. beggars'
   3. house
   4. raft
2. saw, fish, each, give
3. Ping ducked because there were fishing birds dashing all around.
4. A path of crumbs led him to the house boat.
5. He wanted to cook Ping for dinner.

Some Things to Talk About

Answers will vary.

Study Guide pp. 34-36

esson 3
(reading pages 23-32)

ay each word. Write it. Use it in a entence.

nswers will vary.

ead each sentence. What does the old word mean?

. small
. pinkish
. quickly

ill in the blanks or answer in omplete sentences.

. He thought Ping was too beautiful to eat.
. sad
. He heard the footsteps of the little boy.
. The Boy was afraid his father would cook Ping for dinner.
. "La-la-la-la-lei!"
. He marched over the bridge anyway.

Study Guide pp. 38-41

Lesson 1
(reading pages 5-21)

Say each word. Write it. Use it in a sentence.

Answers will vary.

Read each sentence. What does the bold word mean?

1. dangerous weather out at sea
2. always hard-working
3. life stories

Fill in the blanks or answer in complete sentences.

1. Puffin was the name of his boat.
2. He sailed to get medicine for Mama, oil for the lights, and food.
3. She was worried about the responsibility of keeping the lights burning.
4. Her mother was too sick, and her sisters were too little.
5. Three. Esther, Mahala, and Lydia.

Let's Talk.

Answers will vary.

Let's Remember.

Answers will vary.

Just for Fun

Answers will vary.

Study Guide pp. 42-46

Lesson 2
(reading pages 22-40)

Say each word. Write it. Use it in a sentence.

Answers will vary.

Read each sentence. What does the bold word mean?

1. practice writing the alphabet
2. cut the end off of
3. tired of, not interested in

Fill in the blanks or answer in complete sentences.

1. The waves were like big hills.
2. He was away fishing.
3. The first match went out because her hands were shaking.
4. a. blew out each light
   b. trimmed each wick
   c. cleaned each lamp
   d. put in more oil
   e. went to breakfast

Writer's Workshop

Answers will vary.

tudy Guide pp. 48-51

esson 1

ead through "... something to know about."

ay each word. Write it. Use it in a entence.

nswers will vary.

ead each sentence. What does the old word mean?

. walked with heavy steps
. in front
. a. grain
  b. attics

ill in the blanks or answer in omplete sentences.

. the wars
. They did not want to share what little food they had with hungry soldiers.
. This meant they would keep the grain to plant as seeds so more grain could be grown.
. The peasants were pretending they were starving.
. The soldiers decided to make Stone Soup.

ide and Seek

. sacks of barley – under the hay in the lofts
. buckets of milk – down in the wells
. cabbages and potatoes – under their beds
. meat – in the cellars
. carrots – covered with old quilts

ananas and candy canes are not used to nake soup.

ome Things to Talk About

. Brett's horse is fast.
. The soldiers stopped at Paul's house.
. They asked to sleep in Albert's barn.
. They saw the village's lights.

Study Guide pp. 52-55

Lesson 2

Read from "First we'll need ..." to the end.

Say each word. Write it. Use it in a sentence.

Answers will vary.

Read each sentence. What does the bold word mean?

1. cabinet for storing food
2. imagine!; exclamation of surprise or disbelief
3. impressive, outstanding

Fill in the blanks or answer in complete sentences.

1. A fire was built on the village square.
2. They dropped in three round, smooth stones.
3. The peasants could not imagine a soup made with stones.
4. She got the carrots from the bin beneath the red quilt.
5. Marie had cabbages.
6. A table had to be set.

Some Things to Talk About

stones	beef
salt	potatoes
pepper	barley
carrots	milk
cabbage	

Calling All Cooks!

Answers will vary.

Study Guide pp. 58-61
Lesson 1
(reading pages 1-13)

Say each word. Write it. Use it in a sentence.

Answers will vary.

Read each sentence. What does the bold word mean?

1. far away
2. leaves beginning to sprout
3. food which had been planted

Fill in the blanks or answer in complete sentences.

1. She lived way out in the country on a hill.
2. pretty, strong, well, built
3. The Little House felt very happy.
4. No, the Little House stayed just the same.
5. She was curious about the city.

List at least three things that the Little House watched during each season.

Answers will vary.

Study Guide pp. 62-65
Lesson 2
(reading pages 14-29)

Say each word. Write it. Use it in a sentence.

Answers will vary.

Read each sentence. What does the bold word mean?

1. automobile (car or truck)
2. people who measure and divide land
3. train on raised tracks

Answer in complete sentences.

1. The machines were a steam shovel, trucks and a steam roller.
2. Gasoline stations, roadside stands, and small houses followed the new road.
3. No one wanted to take care of her.
4. She missed the field of daisies and the apple trees dancing in the moonlight.
5. She could feel and hear the subway.

Some Things to Talk About: Personification

thought
didn't know
missed
dancing

Study Guide pp. 66-69

Lesson 3
(reading pages 30-40)

Say each word. Write it. Use it in a sentence.

Answers will vary.

Read each sentence. What does the bold word mean?

1. not straight
2. dug up
3. scared

Answer in complete sentences.

1. The large buildings around the Little House blocked the sun except when it was overhead at noon.
2. The Little House dreamed of the country.
3. She didn't like living in the city.
4. She thought it looked like the house her grandmother had lived in.
5. She was jacked up, put on wheels, and moved back into the country.

Country and City

Country - a brook, daisies, dirt road, barn, tractor, apple tree
City - parking garage, trolley car, elevated train, subway, shopping center, street lights

Puzzle Page

oodr = door
foro = roof
dowwin = window
llaw = wall
orchp = porch

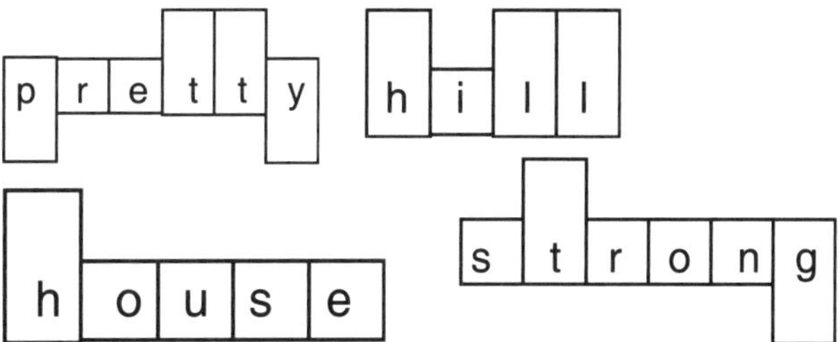

Study Guide pp. 72-75

Lesson 1
Read until "And it was, and she did."

Say each word. Write it. Use it in a sentence.

Answers will vary.

Read each sentence. What does the bold word mean?

1. porch, staircase
2. carved wooden decorations
3. greenhouse (building where plants and trees are grown inside)

Answer in complete sentences.

1. He was a wood carver who made figureheads and Indians. He also painted pictures.
2. She helped him paint the skies in his pictures.
3. Alice wanted to go to faraway places and live beside the sea.
4. He told her she must do something to make the world more beautiful.
5. She hurt her back.

Let's Remember.

Make these possessive:

the jar's lid
the cookies' smell
the children's teacher

Just for Fun

Answers will vary.

Study Guide pp. 76-80

Lesson 2
Read from "From the porch ..." to the end.

Say each word. Write it. Use it in a sentence.

Answers will vary.

Read each sentence. What does the bold word mean?

1. happiness
2. large bags
3. groups of flowers

Answer in complete sentences.

1. She had not done anything to make the world more beautiful.
2. Her back still hurt, and she had to stay in bed.
3. Seeds had been carried by the wind.
4. They want to be careful because she is so old.
5. Yes; she planted fields of lupines. She also encouraged others to do something to make the world more beautiful.

Writer's Workshop

Answers will vary.